Crossings

A Record of Travel

Crossings
A Record of Travel
New and Selected Poems

Michael Jennings

Copyright © 2016 Michael Jennings
All Rights Reserved

ISBN: 978-1-942956-31-0
Library of Congress Control Number: 2016947522

Cover photograph: Alex Noriega
Manufactured in the United States

Lamar University Literary Press
Beaumont, Texas

For Suzanne and Shane

Poetry from Lamar University Literary Press

Michael Baldwin, *Lone Star Heart*
Charles Behlen, *Failing Heaven*
Alan Berecka, *With Our Baggage*
David Bowles, *Flower, Song, Dance: Aztec and Mayan Poetry*
Jerry Bradley, *Crownfeathers and Effigies*
Jerry Bradley and Ulf Kirchdorfer (eds.) *The Great American Wise Ass Poetry Anthology*
Matthew Brennan, *One Life*
Paul Christensen, *The Jack of Diamonds is a Hard Card to Play*
Stan Crawford, *Resisting Gravity*
Chip Dameron, *Waiting for an Etcher*
William Virgil Davis, *The Bones Poems*
Jeffrey DeLotto, *Voices Writ in Sand*
Mimi Ferebee, *Wildfires and Atmospheric Memories*
Larry Griffin, *Cedar Plums*
Ken Hada, *Margaritas and Redfish*
Michelle Hartman, *Disenchanted and Disgruntled*
Michelle Hartman, *Irony and Irreverence*
Katherine Hoerth, *Goddess Wears Cowboy Boots*
Lynn Hoggard, *Motherland*
Gretchen Johnson, *A Trip Through Downer, Minnesota*
Ulf Kirchdorfer, *Chewing Green Leaves*
Janet McCann, *The Crone at the Casino*
Erin Murphy, *Ancilla*
Laurence Musgrove, *Local Bird*
Dave Oliphant, *The Pilgrimage, Selected Poems: 1962-2012*
Kornelijus Platelis, *Solitary Architectures*, tr. by Zdanys
Carol Coffee Reposa, *Underground Musicians*
Steven Schroeder, *The Moon, Not the Finger, Pointing*
Jan Seale, *The Parkinson Poems*
Carol Smallwood, *Water, Earth, Air, Fire, and Picket Fences*
Glen Sorestad *Hazards of Eden*
W.K. Stratton, *Ranchero Ford/ Dying in Red Dirt Country*
Wally Swist, *Invocation*
Lao Tzu, *daodejing* tr. by Breeden, Schroeder, and Swist
Jonas Zdanys (ed.), *Pushing the Envelope, Epistolary Poems*

For information on these and other Lamar Universit Literary Press books go to www.Lamar.edu/literarypress

Acknowledgments

I am grateful to the editors of the following journals and anthologies for publishing some of the poems now collected in this book.

Beloit Poetry Journal
Birmingham Poetry Review
Bitterroot
Bottomfish
The Chattahoochee Review
The Comstock Review
Ekphrasis
The G. W. Review
Prism International
REAL: Regarding Arts and Letters
The Southern Poetry Anthology, Volume VIII: Texas
The Southern Review
Stone Canoe
Tar River Poetry
Vanderbilt Review
Vitruvius

I am also grateful for a Creative Artist Public Service Grant from New York State.

Other Books by Michael Jennings

The Hardman County Sequence
A Dance of Stone
Totems
Ghost Moon
Silky Thefts
Once
Bone-Songs and Sanctuaries, New and Selected Poems
River Time

CONTENTS

Book I: Summoning the Outlaws

Dust and a Good Wind
- 15 Six Tenant Farmers, Without Farms, Hardman County, Texas. 1938
- 16 Woman of the High Plains, Texas Panhandle. 1938
- 17 Damaged Child, Shacktown, Elm Grove, Oklahoma. 1936
- 19 Child and Her Mother, Wapato, Yakima Valley, California. 1939
- 20 On the Great Plains, Near Winner, South Dakota. 1938
- 21 Walking Wounded, Oakland. 1954
- 23 Grayson, San Joaquin Valley, California. 1938
- 24 Toquerville, Utah. 1953
- 25 Man Stepping From Curb. 1956

Before Speech
- 29 Before Speech
- 30 Little Alien
- 31 Squandered by the Hundred Million
- 32 Scales
- 33 Beluga
- 34 Amazons
- 35 Tiger Dance
- 36 The Great Mother
- 37 Black Wolf at Midnight
- 39 One Paw Poised

A Circle of Seasons
- 43 Trees
- 44 Fog
- 45 The Mountain
- 46 March Invitation
- 47 Spring Haiku
- 48 Hawk
- 49 Solstice
- 50 Raccoon
- 51 Always
- 52 October Sun

53 The Road Home, November
54 Ghost Moon
55 December Sun
56 A Moment in February
57 Remains

Summoning the Outlaws
61 *Mon Semblable, Mon Frere*
62 Reading Heaney
63 Drum Song
64 Lowell
65 Talking Bob's Blues
67 Diffusions of August
68 His Mountain Gateway

River Time
73 Alma's House
75 Dancing at the Silver Dollar
76 Skateland
77 Remembering the Alamo
78 Uncle V.J.
79 Bad Men of the Old West
80 Myth
81 Black Elk
82 The Fury of Geronimo
83 Comanche Moon
84 Horse Scapes
85 Ceremony
86 Naming the Lake Wind
87 Invited Guest, Moulin, France
89 River Time
90 Old Man Waking
91 Over Dinner We Begin to Vanish
92 Wolf Song

Book II: the Dark Mothers

95 Ur of the Chaldees, 1958
96 Heat

102 A Dance of Stone
105 Old Mountains
108 For You I Invent the Sun
112 Mary
114 Alex
121 Invocations
133 Vilnius Glimpses
135 Lamentations
138 The Dark Mothers
140 Winter Light
143 Once

Book I: Summoning the Outlaws
Shorter Poems

and I was discovering, naming all these things:
it was my destiny to love and say goodbye.
                    —Pablo Neruda

Dust and a Good Wind

(after the photographs of Dorothea Lange)

A lion does not write a book, nor does the weather erect a monument where the pride of a woman was broken for want of a pair of shoes, or where a man worked five years in vain to build a home and gave it up, bankrupt and whipped...or where the wife went insane from sheer monotony and blasted hope.
        —J. Russell Smith, *North America*. 1925,
          as recorded in Dorothea Lange's notes.

Six Tenant Farmers, Without Farms, Hardman County, Texas. 1938

Dust
and a good wind
will move mountains.

But these are not mountains,
only men. Each stands
with his own hat in his own pose,

and each stares into the blind eye of the camera
with almost the indifference
with which the blind sun stares. Their lives

have come to this. What moves on the horizon
no longer moves them. Like the dust storm's
gray aftermath, they are a stunned stillness

where the wind has been.
                         A dust storm begins
with a single gray particle, dislodged into wind
and looking for home. All heat and hunger,

it owns nothing and so has nothing to give.

What stands in the wind it demolishes.

What it has picked clean it leaves for the living.

Woman of the High Plains, Texas Panhandle. 1938

She stands, her long bones dark against the sky,
one hand on neck, the other pressed to her brow,
and she is laughing, as though out of nowhere
something had just dawned, as though somehow
something besides wind had passed through here
on its way to the mountains.
      Listen:
out here the strained hollow faces of summer
grow stranger in winter, the moth-clouds get eaten
by bats from the north, and the long faces of worry
become the low eyeless dwellings of the horizon,
some small smoke rising from the chimneys.
        Listen:
no one alive shall ever hear this laugh, or see
a woman in a flour sack with the posture of a heron
laugh like a child.
     Behind her the bleak plain
lies echoless, where even the bird-call of her bones
shall die
    under the bright clear rain of the million stars.

Damaged Child, Shacktown, Elm Grove, Oklahoma. 1936

The left eye
is an empty socket. A black stare
into blackness. Behind it: the gray brain that dreams
die back to, like a road map
found on the back seat
of an abandoned car. Shacktown, Elm Grove,
Oklahoma, a place
no one visits, a town that lives
on the rumor of rain.

The smile
is the Mona Lisa's, a vagueness
untouched by vagueness: if one can imagine that
of a half-wit child of eight
who stands in front of four pieces
of dark sheet-metal
that make up the side of a house a child
might throw rocks against
to make thunder.

I once planned
a trip to Nova Scotia, where distance
is decorative. Lakes, rivers: a gentle apportionment
of parts. Four months
went into the planning. It ended
by the side of a road
in a ditch, where a dead dog
grinned and glistened
in the rain.

I carry
a child somewhere in the dark
of my brain. A dead child. She reminds me
of the future. I give her names.
The names change. Today she stands

in front of four pieces of dark sheet-metal
and almost smiles. It is her birthday.
She has just turned eight.
Her one rag

is held together at her right shoulder
by a small knot that is almost a bow.

Child and Her Mother, Wapato, Yakima Valley, Washington. 1939

Her hair is long wet strands of dull black weed.
Her head, heavy with it, is bowed. Her eyes
look toward, but do not see, the ground that lies
like iron at her feet. Her fingers knead
and push the barbed wire fence her body's greed
would fold around. But though the one barb tries
to pierce the flesh, the floral dress despise
its thread, the small belly will not take seed.

Her mother stands behind, hand on hip. She'd
rather she stood elsewhere and not be wise
and know down to her bones that no surprise
will come today, that they will not be freed.
Yet she stands, shades her eyes, mouthing a creed
gone bad, wishing it might be otherwise
than to get up each day to the same skies,
hoping there might be something left to bleed.

But sun has honed their land to bone, and grain
no longer tries to flower. The sky is lead,
the days are long, and nothing in a dream
can change the way their shadows seem to stain
the ground, or make them go, or how the dead
come drifting like the echo of a stream

where no stream flows.
                        So let the body steam
in the long night. Let all the shapes of dread
come welling up in the tired shards of brain
until the eyes of child and mother teem
with murder. No help comes to the dark head.
No black blood's pounding brings the vengeance of rain.

On the Great Plains, Near Winner, South Dakota. 1938

On the Great Plains, near Winner, South Dakota,
winters are long. Philosophy is short.
What goes under snow in November
emerges again in March, sometimes later,
sometimes changed. Life's hard. Daughters
get names like Hope or Faith. Sons
don't get far, or move away
altogether, their letters coming back
full of the emptiness they left with.

And here in the space of what looks like
half a mile, maybe less, three churches stand,
one behind the other, like reflections
of the same church: each painted white,
each with its single black spire
thrust into the northern sky. Nothing else
stands or grows, but the prairie grass
moving away like a whisper.

But distance can be tricky here,
so that the church that stands near the horizon
may be a day's walk, maybe farther. And in deep snow
the situation worsens. Destinations are measured
in yards or feet, sometimes inches. Direction,
too, can be confusing. A man goes
snow-blind quickly in a blizzard, sound
distorts, the mind grows muddled.
                         It is said in the desert
a man never dies of thirst
but he will first see water. Here it is said,
a man never freezes to death
but he can hear the ringing of bells.

Walking Wounded, Oakland. 1954

There is a moment, albeit hypothetical,
when something foreign
         passing through something familiar
leaves only a blackness,
         a record of travel.

                      Blood bulges
     and overruns the hole,
and sometimes a scream flaps out
        from the first O
                 of astonishment,
the face gathering darkness like a hole
        that will never again
                   get quite filled in.

The man in this corridor
     is pure darkness,
                the forest floor,
a black loam you could lie down in
     dreaming of the long rays of sunlight
                       that never come.
     It is dream from which no one wakes.

The man in this corridor
     intrudes
         almost
not at all: a black shoulder, a black pant leg,
     a dead foot and thin line of black crutch
                     angling
from behind a telephone pole.
               There's no body,
     only darkness reshuffling.
No face, only a meeting of moles
     holding silent parley
          in an unmarked grave.

A city is closing
      on the man in this photograph. The telephone pole
looks broad as a door, and the blank wall
      that is the whole right side of the picture
                                looms, somehow,
closer.
      It is washed whiter than any scar.

Grayson, San Joaquin Valley, California. 1938

Say, for a moment, there is this building, too broad
or close for the picture, which looms in the picture
like a bad dream, an image pressed
half on the mind's eye, half onto some darkness
just out of reach.
                    Lines of raw clapboard cross
from frame to frame, while the rooftree, centered,
lets in two triangles of sky: gray, as the building
is gray, but paler, flatter, if anything
more coincidental than the crude structure
that hulks like a bad conscience on a bleak plain
we do not see, but feel, a dull ache of distance
that comes these last miles to lie in the open crawlspace
like a dark stain.
                    And the building hangs like that,
in air, between earth and sky, darkness and sun,
and rivets the eye like a pale scar.
                                        Or say it is a building
built to be come to, built like the men who built it,
who, if they knew little of heaven, knew what they needed
of wood and iron, that is made wholly
of wood and iron, built like a hobnail boot.
                                              And say
dead center in the picture, a man lies, that the building
surrounds him as though he had dreamed it, as though
he had nailed each board. But say he is only
a gunny sack with ankles, a corpse left in the shade
where the rotting is slower.
                              Whether church,
or school, or meeting hall, say it is a building
where men came to listen, its floor and benches
full of splinters, the wind through its boards.
a groaning of iron.
                    Or say the possibilities
run out, that it is a building built by men who spoke prose
and died without fanfare.
                          Say there is this silence.

Toquerville, Utah 1953

Whatever it was, it happened here, sometime after rain
in Toquerville. You walked toward a wall, the progress
slow. It leaned toward you, cracking, as if
trying to accommodate to vague shifts of sunlight
or weather. The scorched air crackled
like an old newsreel (in it men drop like flies, rise
up again, salute and fall back). There was the sound
of rain, a little wind; and slowly the wall took on
a blotchy, blood-splattered look: an enemy wall,
greasy with old deceits, muffled cries.
                                          Then the late sun,
sliding into a window pane, reflected a small path
through the forest, though there was no forest,
only the deceptions of sun in late summer
when the roads, even after rain, stay dusty,
haggard, as from men marching.
                                    You arrived,
flagging, unhealthy. You felt somehow
more like your grandfather: weak-eyed, troubled,
a face forever slashed by a pale blur of sunlight
you are always approaching.
                              Even into twilight.
                                              Turn now
and face this camera full face, the wall
behind you. Remember the evidence,
your grandfather's face: starched, formal.
Remember the patched plaster of faces,
it is all you will ever have to remember.
Remember when the pieces come together
in the cold porcelain of your mind's eye,
it will be someone else's grandfather
who stares out, bland and unblemished,
wearing your face. You will be gone then.
It will be sometime after rain in Toquerville.

Man Stepping From Curb. 1956

This blind black stepping
into gray this gathering
of light around dark
edges this hanging headless
weightless this hungering
for loose hair and wide
thighs this too taut
skin in too slack
air this hope despair this
running through fingers stone
in the hand empty waking hanged
man thief this gathering
of night dispersing
of stars this flapping
in the breeze this anger
this loneliness this wide
emptiness falling into
stars ether this rise
again into ossified
earth this walking waking
dark angel hanging...

Moon forever rising.
Sun forever falling.
Reflect. Reflect.

Before Speech

Before Speech

was the wolf pack, the moon's children,
her insignia borne in the whites of their faces.

There was high ground at the heart of their forest
sacred for long sight, steeped in their smells.

There was bow and gesture, a sniff of the ear
that meant home, that meant heart,
that meant abiding mother with her belly in the dirt.

There was signal flashed across space.
There was the will to sing.
Anyone could start.

Little Alien

Dropped here from outer space,
her eyes infrared scanners,
she wants to be fed and for the world
to go away. She wants to grow feathers
for her star-cruiser
body, to glide the rivers of blackness
she'll come to call home.
In her spaceship egg, she was a whole
galaxy, a liquid listening.
Soon she'll learn about the particle snow,
stealing its white loveliness
as her cold cover. Soon she'll learn about death
under the covenant of stars,

but she will call it life,
chanting her flute-songs of exile.

Squandered by the Hundred Millions

his hell-hunks of rotting flesh
left to slough from his bones
like sacrifices to the god of steel,

one and one and one
he died, she died, they all died,
their stunned unreckoning

rose into stars, numberless as stars.
And the night came
lifting him up with his black rage

and gave him back his magical curving horns,
and lifted his mountainous woolly back-skull
onto the still larger mountains of black woolly shoulders,

and polished his small black eyes
and sharp hooves, his thunderous black bones,
and patched his scraggy, reeking beard.

But by morning the tractors had come
and the grasses vanished, and the dust came,
and that was the end of the first day.

Scales

Old bubble brain
floating in primordial ooze—
turn him on his back
and he sinks into coma,
forgets yesterday, hardly fathoms
tomorrow.

How easily we condescend
in our neocortical glimpse.
He cannot laugh or be sociable.
His one purpose
to go on expanding, to eat
and be filled and eat again.

Mountain ranges grow from his back.
His each scale anticipates
the iron age by eons.
He is the Hindu calendar
written in Braille.
For him it's still the beginning of time.

Expressionless as God.
His undulant tail
the shadowy frond of some first fern
the abstract angels dance on.

Beluga

What were once perhaps arms have simplified in time
to water wings, undulant and white in a black sea
pearled and catacombed with ice.
                                      Pelvis has vanished,
or is at most vestigial, tapering to feet turned tail fin
in a slow fan of somnolent propulsion,
dream-lazy, ghostly.
                        Her call, her only weapon,
is sonar deadly, a stun gun, prelude
to instant swallowing and digestion, death
under anesthetic.
                      The world of stars and sun
and the hard crust of earth
betrayed her, though she visits still,
white in the white moonlight—
                                    the dome of her mind
grown huge and forgiving in the cave of the sea.

Amazons

A pride of 30 lionesses—single
pre-phalanx wall of blond muscle,
pure infantry—slides in one hunger
through the one darkness, patient
as desert wind, insect heat—
slides motionless as the deep sea
stone minded in its one dream
rivered with tendons.
                         What awaits this
in the brush, in the shadow burrows
and ruts of the night wind, must dream
mouths larger than prairies, frieze
in the moonlight nameless as stars
falling—impala become Impala, warthog
Warthog, its riveting shrill shriek
a shearing of metal—
                         night erupting
into bonfire—claws, teeth, flesh,
kin and carcass—mandarin faces,
sleeked in blood, scarred senile
in the anarchy of kill.

Later they'll greet the dawn,
lolling, licking each other, satisfied
they've kept the universe open,
the tall dead rising.

Tiger Dance

She is the languid, languorous
disease of the sun, flower
of his passion, hint
of his corruption among shadows.

He comes to her disguised
as her double, only larger,
more impossibly brutal-beautiful—
his face a Paleolithic sun shower.

She in turn turns tiger lily,
all smiles and pussycat frailty
shivery under his touch—
needier, whorier

than his lewdest imaginings—
his great winking anus
laughing at the winking
gay forest above them.

This is he who has hugged
and scarred the trees
as his vassals, whose gape
at her nape is the very vault of heaven.

This is she
who releases him,
brings on the darkness,
leaves him free again to love nothing.

The Great Mother, After Long Drought

so tiny eyed, so tired, so wrinkle-rivered
in her skin of dust,
has trudged so long in billowing skirts of dust,
knelt fat-assed and humbled as Old Mammy
in chasms of dust—
her great trumpeting trunk following its long instinct
for water.

Now she has come. Leading her cows
into the kingdom of cows,
down long winding rivers of cows,
single-file, dust-smoldering processions—
tusked, vigilant, thunder-shaking—
meeting and touching each
to each in the great milling of cows.

Such soft-handed knowing in that fondling
probing lip! Such fingertip-tender
tickling laughter
behind the preposterously old faces—
Even *elephant* is not word enough!

The rivers are jubilant!
The mud holes grow deeper!
She has come
like a black cloud
bringing a black cloud
to a land like her very skin!

Earth shaker! Bellower! Maker of rain!

Black Wolf at Midnight
    (after the print by Robert Bateman)

At first we do not see the eyes—
bewitched, bewitching—only trees,

their latticework of iced branches
glittering where moonlight patches

the dark, where any moment centuries
old stone cold silence threatens

to crack like ice the thin bark
in the eternal click, click

of minerals in the soft shift of wind.
Some moccasined tracker in skins

crouched under stars, cold heart
in his mouth, might have stared out

and seen, for the first time,
the colossal foot—hairy, snow-rimed—

planted too eerily close. Dread
paw of the wolf feathering upward

to where the gray column of leg dwarfs
the wrist-thick trunks of the light-starved

trees. Then fathomless bulk
of black body and mystic gold

eyes latched onto him there in that
first dark. Ours is the more distant

wonder of Art, that he could do this
so stealthily, shrewdly, our eyes

tuned to these eyes, our gaze
fixed to this stare without remorse

or malice, a criminal angel's—
our shadow brother lost in the ages

light years after.

One Paw Poised

the others planted in snowpack,
here is the lost spirit of the moon's cunning,
joy of the hunt, joy of the kill—

who claimed the gothic conifers
before Goths or Vandals
or the Westward Expansion—

who felt the steel trap's
bodiless jaws, the bullet's
invisible fang; twisted in strychnine

bewilderment—
hung upside down
on iron crosses of barbed wire

and died by the myriad
for our sins.
                Now let us praise him.

A Circle of Seasons

Trees

Today they've come back from the snow—
their dream-walk that began in December—
and are settling in along the ravine
where the creek runs, shaking the fatigue
from their bones, talking softly among themselves.
In a week the elders will speak in tongues.
In two they'll be chanting.
Muskrat will hum.
In a month the blue flower of the lake
will break from her icy spell.

Fog

We woke
to cathedrals
of fog—spires, robes, angels—
valhallas of choral voiced silence.
Its breath obliterated farms,
rode the lake's abyss like a warship.
It took the antlers of trees as its standards.
It marched north along roads
whose cars blundered over ridges
like sleepy cattle. Crocuses
brightened like tiny suns
in the sulfurous galaxies of mosses.
On the second day, it lost pomp and contour.
Drum-silent, it lay moiling over hills in listless aftermath.
It clung to our eye-corners like sooty laundry.
By the third day, the tittering of birds was strange.
Their calls vibrated through invisible holes in our bodies.
Our mouths hung stupidly open—our eyes
merely the shifting mirrors of fog. Our hearing
crept out over fields without hope or longing.

The Mountain

The mountain
at the south gateway
of our glacier lake (still white as satin
in late March) is more glorified hill
than mountain,
                but with the sullen blue presence
of mountain, a sort of brow ridge
thrust up from the softer brown thighs
of the other hills—
                bouldered in Pleistocene sleep,
a hill, like Cezanne's, a man
could walk around for years
and get lost in, his eye cutting
narrow goat paths of perfect
clarity.
        So hill becomes mountain
in a vibration of eye waves, in the forgetting
of tedious plains thrust up out of
sea bottom shiftlessness—
                    leans hard
in the wind, poised toward some moment
it has lost all track of.

March Invitation

Today every tree
a hand of withheld fire
twisted and passionate against the sky—

Rain back to snow, indecisive,
gusts into a sleety, crow-battering wind
combing lusterless scraggy hills,

sifting the sick fields—loam-scent
rising like a witch-brew elixir
from the crushed pterodactyl skull
of last year's robin.

O ravenous mouth making trees shiver,
the black hearts shudder—

If they knew the glad-hand light of summer
working them like a politician full of promises,
how could they forget in their slag-sleep
this whispery touch, this tingling wakefulness
under the dark dreaming magma of sky?

But their amnesia grows perfect again—
O schoolgirls in the hands of the March wind!

Spring Haiku

Easter
in the purple
tulip tree
blooms
goldfinch
yellow laughter
zoom

* * *

Zoom—
yellow laughter
goldfinch
blooms
tree tulip
in the purple
Easter

Hawk

Dark-rumored inkling of air-chills,
pulsing pupils, the whole hill
monastery-still, a tilting
cliff's edge empty
reckoning—blue water, blue sky.

Ponderous, as if in chains,
attended by black birds, he rises
out of the tree-fringe
hoisted by huge shoulders, granite facemask
blank as an angel's

over the flapping canopy of lake
unwavering and undeterred, past lake rim and horizon
into miraculous high noon
where he who owns nothing, not shadow or hunger,
absolves utterly,

becomes nothing—all shadow, all hunger—
the eye-scorching sun unmasked in its bottomless plummet.

Solstice

This afternoon green, angel-winged, shimmering
summer is upon us, a solemn shadowed, silky
sibilant rejoicing of gnats and dragonflies
in heart-throb stillness.

Only the purr of her engines, in full throttle,
disrupts the fish-silence of stars, the Scheherazade
dawn-silvering, moon-mingling, dusk-moiling
blossom of the lake, my son's face

rapt in the reflected bauble of the world.
We fall down like the stars and we die
mutters the machinery of the green woods,
inventing the full weight of the sun,

its canopied light, wing-pulse murmurings.
We rain down like the sun
                              and he smiles, he smiles.

Raccoon

Days past death, he was decomposing
in a ditch by the roadside,
body gossamered by maggots,
haloed by shed, fine fur,
the black swoon of his limbs
grease for the black oil of earth,
his head no longer head
but the mask of an angel's
upward gaze, the shrunk hands
supplicant.
                Out of the murderous
innocence of midnight, he'd come
strolling, with hands of a jewel thief,
eyes of a gypsy—knocked dead
in a moment.
                  The dawn did not mourn him
but lit up the last silvering of his pelt.
The crows pecked at him and savored his eyes.
The maggots swarmed him.
All that pilfering would end soon.
By morning, the curved struts of his keel bone
would house only wind crossing
the leeching black ooze of his emptiness.

Always

under the leaves there was death waiting,
despite your tuned, high-voltage body.

Tigers and rivers glide in us nameless
but the day fades and it is never enough.

The poem deconstructing was an old saw
but we made honey in its warm cauldron

and I said *love* with the white mouth
of the moonflower, with iridescent suns

of coneflowers flaunting whispery black eyes.
It was summer in the garden where you moved

without burden of self like a cloud, paused,
looked, shifting your glorious haunches

like any happy horse claiming its field—
all heat and hunger and applause.

October Sun

Weeks since the sun came. Now its crescendo
dazzles the landscape in a thunder of wind
and flaming holy trees. By four, it's gone—
from gilded hills, wide-skirted valleys.
And we, changed, like boatmen come back
over the sliding gray river of clouds
having looked into fire—we've danced
tipsy under the red-eyed sun. Nothing
so deadly as winter can happen now,
we have sun's promise.
                          And the leaves?
They too have a promise—to vessel
the whirl of his fire
into the whorl of the earth
with no more than a thin mad whisper to go on.

The Road Home, November

Twilight needling the eye—the fogged out,
whited out road collapsing
into goblin namelessness, withering
weird trees, half-light lure
of dog and deer
in the treacherous bearded fields—

Giving in to centuries-old, no-world silence—
head down, nape-of -the-neck
bristling attention
to far star-cauldron nothingness—

Papery-skulled, haggard
from the hard voiced night,
I come to myself
building a fire—webby, ochre light,
oily shadows, elemental
stonehenge geometry of logs, inscrutable
as the star-crossed bones of bison
bruise-blotting the clammy walls of the caves.

Later my son's raw edged ancient crying
and soft-haired nuzzling.

Ghost Moon

haunted by cries on a November afternoon.
The geese, with their compass needle necks,
their tumultuous hurry

are passing, have been passing
for days. Each with a piece of magnetic field
planted deep behind its sun-fired eye

heading south. Jostled by wind, pelted
by rain. *Unlikely, unlikely*
their cacophonous holler, their harpy wail.

Something of us goes with them,
feels the ebb in the blood tides
and salt marshes, the emptiness, the cold.

December Sun

With blank regard, December sun
rides low and lemony
behind the stately spars of the hill trees—
a moment's ambivalence
in the stalled, timeless,
shadowless snow.
                        Crows,
somnolent, creaking, resettle
toward the icier dark
of January doldrums. Old earth
withers behind her diamonds,
under her diadem of thorns.
                                 Despite parade regalia,
medallions and metals, the far trumpeter
will fail and fail
to waken the crocuses.

A Moment in February

It is the light at the center of every cell.
—Mary Oliver

See how the silky sun floods the ermine fields—
ton on ton of sheer white light
tumbling kid-gloved soft—each sun-swooned tree
transfixed, snow mittened, bowed as in prayer.
These are the plains of Xanadu
tilting skyward, the high steppes of the Horseman.
Or this is upstate New York shaken
by the vast pastness of the heart, journeys leading nowhere
but here—sun on the snow, the slurred fur
of feel. And everywhere, tremulous, a shout

that's only the sunlight
ringing the molten hearts of trees.

Remains

My son guides me up the long hill
squelching in run-off, along trails
narrow as goat paths through the trees
to show me the strewn bones of a deer
nested in her shed shreds of fur,
almost golden, where some wood spirit
laid her to rest, and the coyotes
and crows stripped her, leaving only
a hoof and furred knuckle intact
among a clutter of collapsed ribs.
He shows me the clean white vertebrae,
the pelvis with its odd eye hole,
the knee still attached with some last rope
of sinew.   This is his find, stumbled on
as he tried his new spring legs in a downhill,
helter-skelter run, and stopped, and stared,
and in his eleven year old mind knew
that this was the stuff of running
undone, something the receding snow
left for him personally, a sign
of winter's weight.   We eye it together.
We go down on our knees to gather pieces
of the witchcraft mystery. The gray trees
around us are also bones that click
and chatter in the wet wind
of almost spring. The brown limpid eyes
are gone. The crumbling gnarl
of spine, once nerved and tremulous,
is now only a train wreck the grass
will hide in a month's time. We feel
the doorway of earth opening.
We feel the thinness of our skins
and the prickling of short hairs rising.
We know what's at the bottom of things,

how soon the mayflies will be dancing
their measured reels of the evening.

Summoning the Outlaws

Artists Are the Indians of the White People.
—Lame Deer

Mon Semblable, Mon Frère
     for K.S.K.

Old Oily Bones crouching in the Ganges' mud
or sauntering up our drive, Tequila and peppers
proffered like flowers, I feel your shadow
lurking in corners months after you depart—
broken-down Caddy asputter.
                              We drink late,
spout poems and oaths, feel the sun rise
through bleached bones, know the same curse
blesses as the stones are blessed, as Tequila is blessed
and the tongue is a shrine.
                              We swell with the pride
of Flamenco swagger, ride the old blues uncouth
truth and parody, feel the universe
slide through us.
                   You're gone in a swill of rucksacks
and vagabond luggage, crazy patois,
leaving us waving down the drive.
                                  The day
 is full of patches of sun, on the counter,
across the desk, shadows in the gold grass,
as I feel you retreating
                            back into the tall Pennsylvania timber,
head down, long strides, back into the long silence
of unmade poems and gypsy songs.

Reading Heaney

No need to get carried away the voice
says meaning there'll be time enough for that
.
life anyway a slow leak back into
stars from that first edge-of-the-world place

bog-rooted and hedged in cow-quivering sleet
and the imperative to keep weather out

along with such novelties and courtesies
and verities of tongue as horse traders use

language come up to look men in the eye
across the pasture gate and slow reticence

of educated hands attaching fact
to fact all the way back to the Bog Woman

in her death necklace—
                         though the boy looks out
enthralled by the imperative of dawn

to stop thinking to start it all again—
hear the poem knotted up in the sheep's bleat

or the valley's clattering first hooves of light

Drum Song
        in memory of Ted Hughes

The lightning-flashed hag face of the moor
in the torpor of downpour
and the drizzle-dim skull of Heptanstall

and the curse in the blood of the cursed mud
and Heathcliff's Mother-wound horror
put thistle in the tongue of Yorkshire

the crashing shires and long haul of mountains
where rock and wind ate at each other
and ached for each other like star-crossed lovers

fossilized in poems whose undersong
was the silkiest hands of farmers
coaxing at the womb door

and the galloping gaiety of the otter
slipping his pelt like a sorcerer
and the river's unkillable contradictions and seasons

her unkillable children and thunder

in the big double drum of the heart

Eros/Thanatos   Eros/Thanatos   Eros/Thanatos.

Lowell

In the old New York, we said
"If life could write,
it would have written like us."

You lost your arid God, His dragon tail
and gorgeous plumage whipping the sea swell
of your Promethean will and thunder
in your "all percussion" obit for the Quaker—
manner or matter your evolving question—
the boy-Keats muscled to the nearly German.

What then? The down look and the letting go,
whiskey glazed eye in false-gold afterglow,
the soft patter of friends no longer pattering,
snippets, smatterings,
crisscrossed conscience and coincidence,
the world's crush
crumpling in a handkerchief—
as if the daze of old age were all day
in a deckchair's decadent complicity
or child's play.

I like the last poems best, their blurry wonder
and disconnects...
the Boston Brahmin with the southern drawl,
vernacular still sparring for the jugular...
the convalescent back from rehab...
seafarer
come home in a New York cab.

Talkin' Bob's Blues

You can't get there from here though you can go a lot of places
In the switchyard of the mind you can rearrange a lot of faces
But the scent of her hair and the touch of her lips and the curse of her
                                                                  tongue
Say you'll bleed from your eyes till the day you're done

When the plains' red dawns stretch out like lies
And the cut glass of the past gives you spider web eyes
And you feel like you're crawling through the land of the dead
And know the dream of your life should have stayed home in bed

And you don't wanna do what beauty asks
Though she's always there in the mirror's masks
Jean Genet in the role of town crier
Or the vagabond king disguised as vampire

Or the ragamuffin boy who could be anyone
Hank or Woody or the scourge of the sun
Deranging the world to see for the first time
Mississippi was a state of mind
And Desolation just a street sign

You can't get there from here though you jump through hoops
You can dance on the clouds or you can deal from the stoops
Your mama had a sister her sister had a friend
She wanted to bust out he wanted to keep it in
And a baby's cry is the willow's wind
You can't even pray without some kind of sin

Walk down the backstairs slip off in the dark
The devil's face is Joan of Arc's
We might be 40 miles outside of somewhere
But the locals say you can't get there from here

Smoke's been travelin' all through the swamps
Says the trees have been whisperin' the words of *Mein Kampf*

Innocence cries in even the darkest heart
You can die for a rose or you can die for art
And all kinds of things that were wrong from the start

I got a woman behind my door
Says she'll love me but I gotta be poor
Gotta crawl on my knees gotta howl like a dog
But if I'm a prince she'll make me a frog

You can't get there from here though you toss and you turn
And your dreams get heavy and your eyes start to burn
But there's a place you can get to on down the road
Where lying's just another kind of truth in code

And an old man playing a Chinese flute
Says I've had mine you can take the loot
The white beard of nothingness grows from my chin
And the next time we meet we'll all be kin

There's a place I go about a mile from here
Where I take off my face and examine my fear
The lake shines like a mirror and I cup my ear
And nothing much matters but that the words are clear

There are freight cars passing and old crossroads
And dispossessed creeds and broken codes
And dead end dreams where a life implodes
And sometimes you see her dancing in fire
But you can't sing her back from the land of desire

You can bray like a donkey you can caw like a crow
There are some kinds of places words can't go
He went down in the valley to sing his song
And let the echo decide if he was right or wrong

He let the echo decide if he was right or wrong

Diffusions of August

Somewhere, I think, there lurks a poem today—
aching perhaps on the horizon
or in the lost last blue sky of summer.

"I stay indoors and spoil another season"
wrote the old master,
searching the moment within a moment

when the present fades
and there is only the present—
to walk forth crippled thereafter.

Bless us with this curse lisp the thick leaves
with their fat shadows, sibyls
of midnight, silvery wombs of the morning.

The spidery breeze on my face
has come its thousand miles.
The tall trees honor me.

I walk among mountains
and know the angels' names.
I drag my lame foot and feel the beggar's shame.

"They want me to wear old clothes...
not walk in the painted sunshine...
but live in the tragic world."

Hail to thee, dark talkers,
shakers of leaves,
whispering still in the soft air,

in the lazy air,
as insects rattled in the golden blaze
when the poem got made.

His Mountain Gateway
    for Will Hier

All day death hovered—
Coming through weeks of the gray of November—
Becoming the friend
Who would not last the year

And did not last the week.
The lake of his dream
Became a fuming of crystals
And polished obsidian.

The cold deepened and the ice whistled
And the lake thundered
And the scarred ice vanished
And the whitecaps foamed

Till spring became a reflection
Of olive placidity, browns
Transforming to the delicate
Hairy greens

Of a thousand shades and nuances
Before the leaf-loaded abundance
Of summer dreamed
Purple evenings etched in shadow,

His photographer's eye
Honing beauty out of the hard edges
Of weather, season
After season drawn on the lens.

And in the long view south
The mountain named for Song
At the gateway between two mountains
That told us we were home—

The gateway
Where I imagine him still—
His farmer's trudge—
Bull shoulders, dexterous hands—

Casting a warm
But slightly squint eye
On life, on death,
And passing by.

River Time

where *you could see*

*Deeper into the country than you expected
And discovered that the field beyond the hedge
Grew more distinctly strange as you kept standing
Focused and drawn in by what barred the way.*
—Seamus Heaney, "Field of Vision"

Alma's House

I keep seeing this muddy, sometimes sunbaked road
from Alma's crooked porch on the Negro side
of Beaumont, Texas circa 1955.
It's where I stayed when my parents were away,
a world of tumble down shacks and angry
young men that Alma kept at bay
whenever I was out there. Except for Nick,
Alma's husband who sometimes mowed our lawn,
I knew only the women, who took me to church
in their big white dresses and enormous hats
and sang hymns as if they meant them.
Nick called me *Honey* and stroked my hair.
He was the color of dried tobacco leaves
and seemed older and more tired
than any man I'd ever known, but also kinder.
Maybe he'd once been a great hell-raiser,
a razor in his pocket and a bottle in a bag
like men I later met on trains, trading swigs
and stories and a sense of fate
hurtling at us out of the night sky.
But there was no Devil in Nick in my day,
only a kind of fatherly Job.
They fed me mustard greens and collard greens
and okra, dark aromas that made their house
exotic with its tilting floors and peeling linoleum,
and let me sleep in their bed and play
with Alma's nearly blind little black retriever
and Nick's skinny flea-bitten hound, chained
to his house out back. They taught me
to stay out of the way of the gargantuan geese,
the real watch dogs, and to feed the chickens,
and visit Ida, the coffee-colored hairdresser
next door, who'd do all the neighborhood
ladies in her big, hardwood living room
while everybody laughed and Alma smoked
cigarettes, which I'd never seen before.

But I never went down that rutted dirt road
beyond Alma's house that seemed to go nowhere
but into weeds and more collapsing shacks
and maybe some swampland nobody wanted.
When she died I was a freshman in college
and Nick wrote asking for money.
I sent him $10, half my week's allowance.
Sorry, I wrote. Sorry.

Dancing at the Silver Dollar

By day it was a big dreary barn of a place,
but at night it was lit up like stars on the prairie,
the only hot spot in Bandera, a town fed
by dude ranches and tourist trade
with old west storefronts and wooden sidewalks
just like the movies, stores that sold boots
and Stetsons and moccasins, all the attire
of weekend cowboys and cowgirls
who flocked on Saturday nights to the dance hall
called the Silver Dollar, where the steel guitar
sent shivers up your spine like a breeze in the live oaks,
and the women twirled and the men sashayed,
and the sheriff moseyed in with a .38 riding
like a small boat on the fleshy sea of his right hip
as I worked up the nerve to ask the girl to dance
with an outbreak of psoriasis on her right hand
my father said I shouldn't mention and didn't.
She was seven and I was eight—the full extent
of our conversation as we circled the room
doing the two-step, cute as proverbial buttons,
with the whisper of moccasins and the stomping of boots
not quite heaven but close as I'd ever come
to the leathery heart of Texas.

Skateland

was where the beautiful hoods came
with their beautiful-thighed girlfriends
in their dainty skating skirts
and ice-cream smiles.
The chromeless gleam of their late 40s hotrods
blazing in the parking lot,
the iron-polished crease of their levis
more carefully wrought
than any tuxedo pant, they darted
through the crowd with knees bent and hips
swaying to the Wurlitzer burble,
nonchalant as bayou kings and princes
in Lafitte's Barataria tradition—
Dicky Thibodaux with his one glass eye
that made him all the dreamier,
Eugene in his shiny ducktail.
They had a saintlike purity of being
that was steely and lethal.
I longed to be like them—immaculate
and mythical
                    under the swirling lights.

Remembering the Alamo

It seemed half the schools in the state were named Bowie or Crockett
and most of the other half either Stephen F. Austin or Sam Houston.
They were the patron saints of the only religion that mattered
and necessitated a yearly pilgrimage to the Mecca of the Alamo,
there to ponder the great sword of a knife that had made history
on some remote sandbar or other, and the tiny room its namesake
met his end in, there in his tubercular death bed to be shot through
                                                                                        the head
more times than anyone really wanted to count, and contemplate
Crockett's portrait, his almost girlish face and long Tennessee hair
that would have gotten him laughed out of any 1950's bar
in Texas, if not killed. Of course we never imagined the true savagery
of the event, or the suspect motives of the gang of thieves
who wanted to steal a whole country pretty much in the name
of Whiteness. We were true believers. We wanted to step across
a line in the sand, face down thousands, hear our names shouted
like oaths over the blazing green battlefields of our past.

Uncle V.J.

Uncle V.J. lived in a roomy shack a bit off the highway near Vidor,
a more than usually rough neck of the woods in East Texas,
where he kept a passel of hound dogs and fed us the first
and best venison stew I ever had. He wore mustard shirts
(were they also floral?) wide open to the waist
so that the full forest of chest and stomach hair
sort of poured out, this above baggy brown pants
and bedroom slippers he shuffled around in. After dinner,
he'd haul me onto his lap, laughing, mussing my hair,
and promise me a hound pup from his next litter
while my mother squirmed in her chair
and my father cracked out some bourbon to talk business.

Years later I asked him just who *was* Uncle V.J.
Not your uncle, he said. What he was was a timber thief,
and your Uncle Rex and I owned some land up that way
and would try to sell him the timber off it before he could steal it.
He might have been a very rich man, but he'd get drunk
every couple of years and kill someone with his knife
in a bar fight, and then he'd have to pay Percy Foreman
(700 acquittals out of 701 murder cases)
to get him off, and that cost him half what he owned.

Well, I guess half of what you own every couple of years
and you end up in a shack with a passel of hound dogs,
which, so far as I could tell, was just how Uncle V.J. liked it.
They finally did send him up for two years in Huntsville
for stabbing, but not quite killing, his brother-in-law.

Bad Men of the Old West

They are mostly skinny men with big eyes and scuzzy beards
who died ragged in holey socks
with so many bullet holes in their bodies
you can hardly count them,
and yet their memento mori photographs,
in which they are propped up by the grim townsfolk
or laid out in a buckboard or on an undertaker's slab,
startle us with the banality of their quietude
after so much violence.
We have killed here the devil's spawn
the photographs seem to say,
here are the wages of sin,
and we are neither proud nor sorry.
They passed through like any spell of bad weather
and we went back to our commonplace lives
in our kitchens and on our front porches,
and wrote ballads and dime novels about them
as if they were anything but poor angry men gone astray,
imagining them all steely-nerved and remorseless,
pretending we never killed them.

Myth

I visited The Kid's grave around 1960—
neglected, weed-choked, tawdry,
the gravestone squint,
surrounded by a little iron fence
a child could step over.
The nothingness I walked away with
stretched out
into big New Mexican sky.

He got to be the dime novel hero he dreamed of,
though we know only a little of what he did,
desperate in a desperate land, lightning
in the night sky, a singer and a dancer,
stealing fire and taking the consequences.

We don't know what he meant.

2 ¿Quien Es?

In handwriting immaculate
as any gentleman's of his day,
though considerably less fenced in by commas,
he wrote to the governor who would betray him,
I am not afraid to die like a man fighting
but I would not like to be killed like a dog unarmed.

In the end the law was just the other gang,
backed by the bankers, who sent their assassins
to murder him in the dark in his stocking feet.
Death came anonymously as it had
to Siegfried, skewered in the back
in the name of justice.

Black Elk

once rode into battle with only a ceremonial bow
thrust out before him so he became an arrowing
Thunder God, and the blue-coats ran.
Crazy Horse was scarier still, a phantom fire, unkillable.
But the mountains failed them, and the grasses
failed them, and the rivers.
So much Spirit eradicated in 50 years.
So much Sorrow.
So little space to be alone with the alone.
So little time to walk in the sun.

The Fury of Geronimo

His name, associated forever
with relentless destruction, is thought
to have come from his knife attack
on a line of Mexican riflemen
praying haplessly to St. Jerome
once he closed ground
on them.
         They'd taken
everything he loved—
wife, mother, children,
mowed down like grass
in the grass—

and you can't kill a ghost.

Comanche Moon

meant death on the Texas plains, that bone-white light
where the horned, black faced, stone-age
demons of vengeance rode like shadows
of death over the mesas, along trails
few men could trace even in daylight.
They were crueler than the prairies
or the Texas Blue Northers,
crueler than death.
They'd roast you on a spit and laugh,
scoop out your brains while you were still breathing.
They lived so close to the prairie
they were the prairie, it mapped their hearts.
They were magicians with horses,
better light cavalry than Genghis Khan's
Mongols, or the Parthians—
able to tame a mustang in minutes
or steal a horse while his rider slept, one rein
tied to his wrist.
                    But in the noonday sun
the bleached bones of their buffalo
stretched farther than the eye could see,
their ponies murdered by the thousands.
They learned no pitiless savage sun god
could ever match the intricacies
of Christian hypocrisy
or the murderous Comanche
that grew in every Texan heart.

Horse Scapes

Remington's bronze broncs are curs,
each renegade muscle
the bulge of a new start
demanding blood. His rider
is Poseidon taming the waves,
his hat a flagrant tool
and insignia,
wind-creased and nautical.

The Indian ponies are more soulful,
painted into the plains like desert flowers
or whirling dust storms.

Under it all, behind it all—
mesa, arroyo, castle rock or butte—
in splendor or bereavement,
the ancient dirt.

Ceremony

Tonight black skeletons of maples against a November sky
is all I know of heaven and all I hope to know.
Russell Means is dead. Geronimo is dead. Crazy Horse
is dead. And in the land of the sacred outlaw
Obama has taken the White House.
Viva Zapata and his white horse.
Viva the snake-eyed killers of lies
and those who stand in line.
Tonight under the long ache of distance and far stars,
I celebrate ghosts whose moccasined soles
listened to earth, the great mystery of trees,
coyotes yelping on a black hill.

Naming the Lake Wind

Perhaps a word on her lips—
intimate for soft fingers
furred and purring
with the overhead flirting of leaves

but something steely too
for its whiter white of winter
a knife all blade
and blare—
skeleton fingers

or the black-fletched
buffeted crows with murder voices
and arrowing cries—

someone with moccasin soles stitching mountain
to valley
to lake stream
and granite

lending some name to the ghost of her spirit

    (For Susan Deer Cloud)

Invited Guest, Moulin, France

The Charolais cattle in field after tree-fringed field
in the late light
were mammoth white boulders of marbled muscle
and food for the gods.
They had no word for the cruel centuries
or the bellowing betrayal of abattoirs,
and so grazed happily
in their sun-blessed tonnage.

The 16th Century monastery-turned-hotel,
where I lost my room down labyrinthine passageways
long past midnight
and a marvelous Beaujolais,
had three blood-red roses atop the high ivy wall
opposite my window
I imagined planted by someone quiet
and close to God.

At night the church bell tolled the centuries,
and silence in the fields
was blessed by morning fog.

* * *

Some of the Siberian Huskies I judged
showed in their slant eyes and long muzzles
the last remnant of European wolf
slipping his skin
and going domestic several generations back.
I felt him like a ghost under the groomed coats
and clipped nails
and man-smell, and felt holy.

And then I met myself coming and going in airports
and among the burnished clouds
at 30,000 feet

and the sweet sad dream of Icarus—
my face in the blank video screen
colorless and baggy
near the end of its time, that was no time at all,
bringing me home.

River Time

The hills are green with summer,
the lakes cobalt blue and glittering.
Whatever we longed for in March
is here already or forgotten.
Your hair gleaming obsidian
as always, despite a few white renegades,
your body stretches out like a great cat's
or a landscape I never tire of crossing.
When I kiss the small of your back,
I hear the whisper of desert sands,
the rush of young rivers. No one comes back.
No one steps twice in the same body.
Spring was sun on the daffodils
and the time of the new wide sky,
the heart-breaking golds
of the giant willows.
Marry me, marry me
shouted the cardinal in his tall tree
while the goldfinch giggled
I am nothing but light.

Old Man Waking

Old age is all right, a little blurry, not dark yet
but getting there, and everything suddenly
a theft from somewhere else, and the laughter
of Rembrandt's last self-portrait.
Maybe it was all a mistake. Eventually
you're everybody anyway, with dreams
real as childhood's, and other things
held more skeptically apart
and dream-whimsical
against, I guess, the coming dark.
I shuffle and limp and talk to myself
less. I calculate before I move.
I dream of being young.
Emerging from heart surgery, I learned
how the body wars for itself
until they strapped me down,
and how when the earnest moon faces
asked if I could speak, I could not.
Next morning I woke in a desert
town abandoned, blighted, old sheds,
whispering sand. It felt like home.
I heard the cement mixer shush
and crackle of great hooves forging
through flaking, crumbling stone,
saw massive knees churning.
I knew it was Rakhsh, Rustam's steed,
breaking from the mountain.

Over Dinner We Begin to Vanish

Let me not to the marriage of true minds
Admit impediments.
—Shakespeare

The faces behind our conversation
begin to sag.
In hard light we look bad.
We know what was.
We laugh.
Soon knowing won't matter
and the moon will rise.

* * *

The moon will rise
into the twin
obsidian lakes of midnight,
one water, one sky, owls
chuffing their bloodlusts. Two pools
suddenly bottomless
will wake in one another's morning.

* * *

We'll wake in one another's morning
with Coyote's cunning,
Raven's black laugh,
a whole day to do mischief,
shuffle the sign, bend the law,
eons to rearrange
the faces behind our conversation.

Wolf Song

I come back to the river,
my tail plume light as a feather
in feathery wind.
I am the stones' ancestral voices.
I am the wide earth listening.

My girl is my playmate
in a song of Hafiz,
quick feet to feed our children,
eyes the color of spring rivers.
See our quick feet dancing.

Red sky. Rock ridge. So I travel
and the gold sun honors me,
singer of high places, queen night,
sifter of pheromones.
I scent the leaves and my good bones marvel—

lordly in the far off
nearness, the arrow and the bow.

Book II: the Dark Mothers
Longer Poems

This day departs. It was a seed
of cold light that returned to its pod,
to its dark mother, to be reborn.
　　　　　—Pablo Neruda

Ur of the Chaldees, 1958

They are like aliens on the moon, the Americans—
bermuda shorts and cameras, pudgy, pale,
a little queasy from the train ride.
Dust from the storm in the night
has permeated everything they own
down to the skin.
They are not quite certain why they came,
and wear the baffled, blinking looks of baby birds.

The hole in the ground is the biggest I've ever seen,
with "evidence of the flood"—a four foot wide ribbon
of sand half way up the sides of an otherwise brown pit
strewn with broken bits of pottery. Local kids, urchins,
scamper down the steep, thin path at break-neck speed
for *rials* and *dinars*. They seem to have sprung up here
without benefit of parents or care. Across
the millennia, I feel the closeness of children
and the terrible price of money.

After a long climb, I am first to reach the summit
of the ziggurat
and so enter the dusky sky of Abraham.
I am 10. My heart is a drum.
I stand at the top of the god-forsaken world.

Heat

Day without plot. Fixtured and fissured. Fractured beyond measure.

I have known heat to stretch horizon to horizon
Like bright steel—a metal or mica or star-scattered heaven
Foundering the mind. Thick-tongued and wordless. White sand
On black brain. Blood rivered in suet. A pocket
Picked empty as wind.
                              Nothing moves in such heat,
Not lizard or scorpion, sandfly or shadow. Tree
Becomes rock, becomes gray husk, becomes
Ruinous. Squalor of sand. Numbness of sun.
                                           To squat there,
The stones of your absence in your hands,
Is to squat in the center of silence forever.
It is to hold the sun like water in the crumbling of your hands.

* * *

It is to hold the bright day. Sun. Sand. A dun-colored dog

Disappearing into a distance of sun and sand—
Humped, slavering. The steady
Rise and fall of the four flickering paws
Too maniacally silent and concentrated for even
The loose gesture of wind to intrude on.
                                       Or the dream of the day,
A child's sorrowing and dreaming—aftermath
Of that too much excitement. Four boys with baseball bats
Who had braved what they knew of the horrors
Of the desert, a compound of mad dogs
And oil drums,
            barbed wire and heat,
A dun-colored dog disappearing into desert like a dead wind.

* * *

It hangs like a daydream of fish in the sun's eye. Fish flying

Like birds above the thunder of dynamite, burble of river,
Then falling to flotsam. Fish by the armload,
Blind, dazed, flaccid as faith. A stench
Ripping open the whole length of the gullet of sky
And left for foxes and flies.
      A day I walked in sun
Unstable as the dynamite I carried in a brown paper sack
Like in indigestible lunch.
      And threw. And walked. And threw.
And watched the shards of hillside rise
Like torn brains to hang in the hair of scrub-trees
While the lizard sang silent in the sun—the blood-
Throated lizard, bloated and bragging in the swaggering sun.

* * *

Or the daydream of glass. White light. Bone light. The sailing of glass—

Shards of pottery heaped in domes
Where ziggurats grew round in wind
And the tombs of kings
Stunk with centuries of fox.
      The sun was a blind mad eye
Carved on an obsidian stairway to heaven
Where the fallen bulls of stone
Offered their great backs to me to ride
And dust filled the air like glass.
      Mother's eyes were black fires
As she hurled ashtrays and plates, bowls and crystal
At walls and mirrors. Her voice
Was glass breaking. Her breath was ether.
      The stench of fox,
Like the burning of flesh, stayed in my nostrils for days.

* * *

A dream before I knew you, met you. Though I knew of your absence.

I knew of Lydia Cathcart who spread her great thighs
On the Riding Club couch or across
The great outcropped boulders of the desert
For grooms and stable hands.
                            I knew of her husband's
Straw-colored pomaded hair and creased
High-fashion trousers,
                    and how her eyes bugged out a little
And spittle formed at the edges of her mouth.
                                  Akbar,
Who would die in the advanced stages of syphilis,
Served out drinks and food, laughed
Like a girl, and kissed me when he could.
I knew of your absence. And I dreamed of Lydia Cathcart.

* * *

And of women on horseback—long shadows in the deep hills.

And one who rode a stallion like a black wind
That even I could not ride,
                        her hair a raven black.
And then the horse who fell and bled for me,
A deep pocket of blood forming between his forelegs
Like a breast—
              a black horse with a girl's mane
And a king's name.
                  And then the dream of women
Ridden by men or boys
In the twilit paddock, moving
Down the long hill in the long heat, arm
In arm, indifferent to all but the long loneliness
Of the first stars rising,
                      the glittering of raw, fierce weapons.

* * *

And the desert rises then in the twilight. It lifts

Its burnt body out of itself. The scabs of its flesh
Soften. It sings in its silence like an old woman
And becomes young again.
       Her sands glitter in moonlight.
Her ridges rise like deep rivers entering the sea of stars.
Her foxes find new stealth,
      their fur bristles.
Snakes slither from dark dens with eyes like stars
And tongues like the singing of stars.
       This is the clarity
Of fire.
   This is the clarity of the long bones of the hills
Rubbing together like the thighs of the long woman
Buried among them.
      This is death.
This is the white-hot crotch of death, blue as a diamond.

* * *

And Gafoor smokes his hookah with yellow eyes. Rocks

And claps his thighs. Dreams himself. Stinks of horse,
Stinks of women, stinks of the sun and the sun's lies,
The long ride.
     And the round stones of the moonlight
Are the hunched backs of the night's feeders
Who rise and walk—
      Or the arched bellies of the night's
Eaten. Who do not get up. Who turn on themselves
Like sculpture. Blue stones.
       And the tarantula
Rising like smoke
     sings to his green-eyed mate
Under the arched light of her dark sting,

And dances there in the round light.
                                        Long night.
The yellow-eyed. Soft-thighed. Torn and turning.

* * *

And then shard-light in the broken east and the stones' cry—

The huddled bones,
Carcass and carcass. Confession of sand,
Celebration of wind.
                        And bright blood blooms in the desert
As the blind white fish
Flounder from withered pond
To withered pond
Where once the river flowed hard
In the moonlight.
                    Achilles died
That Odysseus might live—the heartless heart
Succumbing to the body's stealth,
                                    the moon-fired fox,
Skulking and singing, meeting the dawn's dead eye.

* * *

O daughter of days. Mother of nights. If I have sought women

As the sun
Seeks water,
            eye
In eye,
        tear
                and muscle,
                            forgive me the long chains'
Shackle and shackle. Forgive me the great bull-bones
Of the world in the sun,
                        and hold me now in the implacable
Pallor of your gaze, this improbable poise

Of full moon at dawn's edge—
      Bone-song,
           wind-haunt,
Voice of the fathers
And the father of voice—
      Bring back
The great wind,
    sing me the singing,
        the great song—

O blood of the mothers who labored long!

A Dance of Stone

Whoso ascribeth partners to Allah hath wandered far astray.
They invoke in His stead only females; they pray to none else
than Satan, a rebel...As for those women who are found guilty
of lewdness...confine them to their houses until death take them.
(From the *Surah* of the *Qur'an* entitled "Women")

For six long days they've surrounded my house—
these fat, squat men crouching upon their hams,
having their food brought out to them—eating,
leering, and licking their thick fingers. Six
long days. And on the seventh, I shall die.

I can remember how my father knelt
for hours before the stone goddess, a hard man.
And when he took me in his arms and squeezed,
I wished, sometimes, I too were stone. At night
he loved my mother hard. From where I lay,
I'd see her face grow larger and more craven
until, at last, she'd scream. Her face grew calm
then, calm and small, like that of the stone goddess.

The night of the long scream, when the men came
with large, torch-lit faces and killed my father,
I didn't cry. My mother screamed and her face
grew large. And he was small then, small and broken
like the stone goddess. But I didn't cry.

And then the men with torches and large faces
took me with them, and, for a time, were kind.
They told me of a strong god who was kind
to women, merciful they said, because
women were weak. And as I grew older,
they came to me at night and brought me gifts
and told me how my breasts grew large. At dawn
they cursed me, saying it was they who were weak.

I grew distrustful then, though never showed it.
I took their gifts: this house, the serving
man they gave me. Agreed, also, to consort
no more with the good women of their tribe,
but only with this single serving man.

And still at night they came to me with gifts,
but spoke no more about their strong, kind god.
Once, in the night, one brought my father's goddess—
charred, broken—saying how I might mend her.
I cried then, cried for having once forgotten
how small she was, and broken, and but half
understood—cried in words I hardly understood.
And the years passed. And still at dawn they cursed me.

At last, this six days past, the elders came
and cursed me then in earnest, said my house
was Satan's house and my gods Satan's gods.
They took my goods, my food, the serving man
they'd given. When they left, they locked the door.

I screamed then, tearing at my clothes, my hair.
I clawed great furrows in my face and breasts.
And feeling how my own blood ran, I cursed them—
cursed just to see them there, squatting and leering,
having their food brought out to them. At first
I cursed only in their own blunt, thick tongue.
Later, in the smooth language of my father.

At this they laughed and jeered and threw small stones.
I saw their hatred then, their fear, and I screamed
louder and longer, cursed until I fell
exhausted. Then they laughed again and asked
what good my father's stone could do me now.

Becoming calm. I went deep into my house,
far from the shouting and the stones. They fear
this silence, I said, fear my stillness. From me

they want only some mad, lewd dance, not quiet—
they do not want me dead, only to die.
And I took up my goddess, spoke to her
and made her whole, finding what I had half
known, half forgotten—the stone goddess dances.

Tomorrow, when they enter into my house,
they shall come quietly, afraid, as if
into a shrine. And I shall dance for them—
dance of my father and my father's people—
a strong dance, a good dance, a dance of stone.

Old Mountains

There were mountains in the old place,
the place of old bones, and the mountains
were like bones, only browner, sandstone,
though sometimes bleached pale as bones.
And dark goats moved among them,
and the people who grew out of them
were like goats, small and dark
and quick when the sun was not pure
poison, moving about their business
which was not our business, theirs
being soil, which there wasn't much of,
ours being oil, which came out of the ground
by the ton and snaked through the hills
and desert in pipelines inevitable
as the azure, steel sky itself. Perhaps
they were not real mountains so much
as up-thrust foothills, craggy plateau
a man or goat could climb in a day,
stand at the top of, and feel Moses
come down from.
                    They were holy mountains,
and under the holy mountains was oil
that sometimes still made bushes burn
or the Red Sea part for the islands
of deep-bellied freighters, pregnant
with crude.
               And if they were not mountains,
they were at least the high steppes
of the horsemen, grown ghostly with time,
and my sleeper's body slept among them,
and my dreamer's body, which was only smoke
from village chimneys in winter, or the black
eyes of the skulls of their huts in summer,
saw the quick shimmering emerald of the fields
and crevices in spring, the flash of the bright-dressed
girls of the waterhole, their ankle bracelets

saucy as the glitter of crime in Salome's eyes,
and the black eyes under the black wind
of the black *chadora*
billowing around the husks of crones.
They were the sacred mountains camped
at our outskirts, while our fathers
mined oil from beneath them and hardly
saw them.   But their graves sang to us
in the evenings, and the thin smoke
of their cook-fires rose like ghosts,
and they lay down with us in our dreams
like beasts, breathing and patient.
                              "Ours,"
we thought, as the Persian blue sky
swaddled their shoulders, as the black
night sky lay down on their backs
with its pinprick stars. They rose
like continents in the black sea
of nightfall, then rose again like the skulls
of sacrificial beasts in the dawn. And perhaps
our white mothers heard them and started
drinking harder, savaging the servants,
quarreling with our sad sack fathers.
Distracted in the midnight, they paced cold tiles,
their bare feet lisping the hours—
ethereal, haughty, silken whisperings.
And the mountains were theirs, too,
and the dirty hands of the servants
who needed such scolding. Some absence
lurked in their eyes like the shadows
of mountains, among the coffee klatches
and beer-swilling mornings.
                              But we
were the children of the mountains,
and they entered us as easily as sky,
as easily as night, and what they showed us
was fire and shadow, dancers under the worn moon.

And we saw how time moved in ripples toward the horizon,
shuddering under the noonday sun. They moved
in us like the spirits of Alexander or Herod,
Nebuchadnezzar, Ashurbanipal, Xerxes
or Artaxerxes—slow fires
in the waking midnight.
                                      And our incongruous
fathers waited at the bus stop—white,
short-sleeved shirts, clip-on ties
and crew cuts. They talked of Oklahoma
or L.A., Atlantic City or Baton Rouge,
but never of the bleached mountains
on the hem of whose skirts they stood
dazed in the morning light. Their gaze
was too calculated, the sheaves of paper
in their briefcases too diagrammatic
and impersonal. Children of the Depression,
their souls had suffered foreclosure.
They had bankers' eyes.
                                They are mostly
dead now, copies of *Forbes Magazine*
strewn on the night table. And we
who were children of the mountains
search nightly on the News for glimpses
of the pale, pitiless sleepers—there
behind the reporter with blank banker's eyes,
beyond the rolling dust of tanks, bomb blasts
and squalor, the rubble of apocalypse.
We have joined the absent ones.
Nothing there now remembers us but the mountains
etched behind our eyelids.

For You I Invent the Sun

1.
This, of course, is what money won't buy, this
hip-to-hip, two-centered circle, drift
and drift—you in front, provocative
as a pomegranate, me in front, hearing
echoes—your footsteps filling mine
the way perhaps snow fills the tracks
of caribou, keeping the wolves off. We're
birds of a feather. Our minds veer
and arc on the same air. It's open season here
on sun and wind, and I'm wearing my license
conspicuous and on my sleeve.

2.
We scuff and boot the leaves like six-year-olds,
grin like raccoons. *These are years,* we say,
*shed like snake skins—doomed, irrelevant,
beautiful.* Miles or years, we've walked
forever here, you and I, putting on
or shedding each other like light or leaves,
the traffic hushed and distant. We feel exotic
as the names of these lakeshore towns we walk in,
the water quiet, leaves falling, the light quixotic.
It's all new. You're new—taut and muscular
as a spring colt claiming his first field.
I'm new—grinning ear to ear, hearing windmills.
Death is new here, too, and moves like water underfoot.

3.
We drift in October light through the rose garden,
all the roses gone. Clothed in purple and black,
you're naked. Naked, raspberries and cream,
you're clothed. It's magic. For you I invent the sun,
feel tragic, drive it to your doorstep
in a long yellow cab, stand there, hat in hand,

like some foolish figure in a thirties' flick—
your hair darker than any back row seat.

4.
You talk, stoop, pick weeds, say *the sky
has breadth*. I say *birds have scissored
it to death,* but I'm dazzled anyway.
It's late fall. The birds look hungrier.
You say you're leaving your husband anyhow—
for all his good, for all my bad.
Standing against a tree, your hood up,
your half-moon smile floating somewhere
below the hairline, I imagine you grew there
whole, yesterday perhaps, dew-like, and I
kiss you, feel shy, boyish—hungry
the way the old birds must
who won't get south.

5.
It's mid-winter and the crunching underfoot
sounds rare, precious. You're
purple and yellow. I'm fatigue L.L. Bean
gray-green. The six years between us though
is hardly May and January,
and I'm dazzled by purple and yellow
and can outrun you anyway.
You admit now, though, cold hurts,
for all your tough talk. I should admit
what...for all my tough talk?—that my wife
writes, calls, cries, argues, accuses? Indeed
this crunching underfoot *is* precious—glass
or ice. It's January. It will soon
be May. Our rooms are white and beautiful
and bloom with plants.

6.
Your mother calls, sends chocolates, prays—
makes me feel like the anti-Christ. And

it's true enough I come from a land
of sand and stone, and never put much trust
in trees or green. (In my mind's eye
I always return
to the same rock ridge, almost abstract now
in the blind revision of its lie—
a dark saw-blade raised against blue sky.)
But here, your walk is so much like the sun
or prayer, I must stoop
and touch the place you've stepped, knowing
come spring, something will grow there.

7.
Today bright sun makes blue sky and white birds
pure blue, pure white, barely visible
as we squint and almost stumble
in the pure light.
      Yet we feel entitled here
as tourists, say, who've paid their fare,
though never dreaming it would look like this.
Beguiled by the low cant of foreign tongues,
we're half afraid some blunt truth in our own talk
will startle us back to earth, bring the dream
crashing like glass about our ears.
          But this
is mid-March,
    when the wind blows and the domed sky
holds,
  when small nests of clustered stones
nosing into wind on the iced canal
rise and become birds.
       This is the season
of the long white distance,
      when seeing
is much like blindness, blindness like pure sight.

8.
You say, *You are the magician, I but the source.*
Who could top that? Who, mid-stride,
could help but feel the joy
of fear stutter his heart
like cloud-shadow. We have walked
a long time. It is growing dark. I wish
to take you in my arms. I wish to say
to the child we will one day make,
*you grew here, among sun and wind
in the gathering dark.* I wish to say,
*your mother was taken for goddess
among stones, among these circling
and calling birds,*
                        and they were not far wrong.

9.
We have, I think, no word for this thin-aired
quiet full of light, through which we drift
like new ghosts
risen to Elysian Fields—the still, green lakes
somnolent as deep thought. It's the day
before Easter. The fishermen
standing on the firm bank
wave their fly-rods like bright wands
toward dark depths
where once new life must have climbed, sloth-like
into a dream of sunlight,
and where now loud children and willing dogs
are all smiles, wagging tongues,
sinew and muscle.
Today we talk less, think more.
Today we smile at all that is sensuous
and literal.

Mary
(1901-1991)

In that city of black iron lace and Gullah talk,
sin sashaying in shadow, I see you walk
down Pirate's Alley, the quick click of your heels
too Episcopal for the tolling of St. Louis's twelve-tongued bells—
a tea rose in a carnival of azaleas—
white-gloved, sky blue, crisp as your forbearers of East Anglia
yet frankly forgiven in the not quite sultry air
of Easter, taken in by the wide river-mouth patois
of slithering shadows on darkened stairs
in just glimpsed courtyards

and swallowed whole in the black rivers of music,
sirening souls, palaces of jazz-joy, the air thick
with spangled night. A slur of voices
and footfalls on the wet-black streets poised
in mid-summer. Bourbon, Decatur, great
boozy names rolled deep in the throat—
a swill of voices
like the night's breeze, tropical, luscious.
And yours in the plush garden of wrought-iron chairs
crackling like a voice on the wireless—
matter-of-fact as a boot sole,
yet fluttering, fluting its thrill
of the just-so.

You were my first mother in that city of flowering nights
and sweating patios. Duplicitous, cunning,
sometimes mad as a hatter,
you undermined your own daughter
to hold me in the tight
niche of your charms—there where Lafitte
strode and Napoleon's death mask
stared ceilingward, I see you flash—
old outlaw in a city of outlaws,
sainted in a city of saints,

"queers," "reprobates." You gave me awe
and madness, a taste for all things stained

and fallen.
You were my New Orleans,
your chasteness the flip-side of the stripper's martyred gaze,
the sagging wistful gays
your courtiers, the wisteria your bloom.
Mary, they called you. Mary of the crossword puzzle and afternoon
tea, Mary of the rocks, Mary of situations,
whose fall from grace—divorced, shunned,
a bastard grandson and a strident, quick-tongued daughter—
was resurrection in a place of flowers

and music, of terraced talk
on the floating hills of passing nights.
I learned to walk,
your hand in my hand, your electric
voice in my ear.
Even over years, your letters came with the same click
and stutter, your "Angel" signature the relic
of some old family joke
I never quite got.

"The Velvet Bulldozer,"
your doctors whispered near your death.
Your shingles punished you for years,
your retinas detached, your hearing failed.
Only your mind kept ticking in its queer act of will.
In the end, you were vituperative and genteel
as any southern belle. Nurses scuttled.
Doctors deferred. But even their regard
could not hold you forever.
You died with a small sigh—

white in a whited field.

Alex
(1929-2001)

1
No act of will or Psychic Hotline cant
can raise you from the "utility urn"
I bought you in from Jern's Crematorium
last week. You're done, Mom, and you shan't
correct my English, nor nothing rail nor rant
against forever more. No high-dudgeon
antics can stir the pot. Not even Nieman
Marcus on credit card can make you less than spent.
Farewell to the 12 Minton place settings
you never used, and to the Stickley bed
big as a Roman bath—to the nightshade
and St. John's Wort, masseuse, bed-wettings,
panic calls, blindness—all that pricey dread—
and those who promised love that never came.

2.
You were of course the damaged princess, downed
at seven by the osteomyelitis
in your forehead—surgery, leeches,
one eyelid frozen, headaches that would pound
and pound until you saw yourself as drowned
and then redeemed in your own helplessness.
Great doctors mumbled over you like priests
until the divorce lawyers came and found
your miscarrying mother drug addicted,
your rich daddy a secret queer and crazy.
The baffled judge at last left you to choose.
You were just 10. Your breathing grew constricted
and the courtroom walls leaned in. You told me
how the strange tears splashed on your new red shoes.

3.
And so you chose the mother you would hate
by 17, who stole your friends and lied
and put on airs, while the new poverty tied
you to yourself like a bad smell. Late
to work one morning in the Gulf Coast heat
after a six mile walk, you were mortified
to find deodorant on your desk, tied
up with a little ribbon of pure hate.
That was the day, perhaps, you swore off sweat.
Powdered, perfumed, your beauty cool as ice,
you wore a long red coat, stiletto heels.
When, like soft wind, you tucked me in at night
and whisked away into a world of eyes
and mouths and random men, I felt your steel.

4
I hear your sniff of violated privacy
as my man's hands riffle the soft innards
of your long bureaus—folded, layered,
immaculate, lush femininity,
but not quite lacy—wombs of secrecy
that hold old letters in frayed ribbons, half-heard
snatches of conversation like the words
of little girls whose coy hypocrisy
you loathed. Was it your father's shortness made
you crave tall men, with timber in their voices,
who glowered down at me like men on stilts.
Was it just irony the man you married
stood only five foot six and favored boys.
Still I hear the venom of your hissing silks.

5
"Jarvis, Elizabeth Alice," your great
grandmother, slips from a bottom drawer,
faded but lovely as a long-pressed flower,
at perhaps 17. I contemplate
her unstrung collar. She was maybe late

to come in for the photo session hour,
her hair windblown, a breathless now or
never slight parting of the lips. Her fate
was to become an itinerant schoolmarm,
revered for high intelligence and wit,
who married a young minister and raised
three daughters of a certain bearing, charm,
humor and piety. What doesn't quite fit
the story, though, are her eyes—wild, slightly crazed.

6
What tamed that wild gaze that did not tame yours—
the cold Michigan farm?—anxieties
by candlelight?—the sleepless ministries
to endless household needs? From bottom drawers
they all come tumbling out, the ancestor
church ladies. Your grandmother's diaries,
chock full of weather's cheery godliness,
tell nothing of herself, only her prayers
to better serve. They warmed the glittering ice
of those heartbreaking farms that made you cringe,
if family jottings be believed. White haired,
bleak boned daughters of the mad-eyed Alice,
they show up faded at the faded edges
of family picnics—wistful, shyly proud.

7.
Your existential loathing of the family
tree came early. One minister seduced
proved quite enough. Even old "Elder" Brewster
of the Mayflower hung there in the leafy
branches your mother grew like Blake's Poison Tree.
Its roots were Charlemagne and Robert Bruce,
the Black Douglas and John of Gaunt. No half-truth
was squandered in her quest for ancestry
of might and merit. You were the poor daughter
who'd never measure up to that high-flown bunk
and didn't try. You sang your own mantra.

You were no Mary Ann, let alone "Junior."
You were no pious chip off the old stump.
You changed your name to Alexandra.

8
Not the carpool mother who sang I Like
Ike songs. Not the girl damaged by her father
who could not say no but not quite yes either.
Not she who made little me one May night
with a blond Mick prize-fighter without quite
conceiving what went on in the weeds there.
Not the petulant, angry daughter,
or even the bad mother or bad wife.
You wanted to exist uncategorically.
You wanted to be an original
created in the diamond moment. Not
for you the pain of being only
one woman. You desired to be impossible,
and stirred and stirred and stirred and stirred the pot.

9.
You loathed your mother's wheeler-dealer lies.
She worried you could *be* but could not do—
and always two stories of what was true—
yours and hers, hers and yours in perfect symmetry—
her outward quest, your inward journey,
clashing like cymbals. Both your winds could woo
me. I just saw varying shades of blue—
you darker and she lighter, but the same sea.
You both loved words, and words kept you apart.
In the same room, I'd feel your grinding wills
like creaking oarlocks, both a little crazy
and both killed off by the same bad heart.
You read Proust. She read me Wordsworth's "Daffodils."
In different climes, you each got called "a lady."

10
You toyed with me with threats of suicide
that year I turned 11. Even then
I thought you were just putting me on
at least half the time. But of course I cried
and rubbed your back, and in my own way tried
to wrestle down your darkest demons
as if you were my double. And just once
I feared you'd kill me in my sleep—some tired
hotel in Switzerland as I recall.
We'd fought. You had been drinking pretty hard.
But I remember mostly how the lake
was blue as lapis and we were immortal.
The incident left us drifting apart.
We just let it alone for beauty's sake.

11
All family wars play out best with three.
"What can we do with Alex, what's anyone
to do with Alex," Grandmother would intone
when I was fourteen and thought life easy.
We'd settle in for a long night's breezy
confession of your sins. Crazy as a loon
sometimes, she had the storyteller's one
virtue—to forge some actuality
just as she forged diplomas that got her work.
You were the poor poet of introverted
glances, who saw not things but in their ideas
that fluttered mothily toward the Absurd.
For you communion lurked behind the words.
After dissecting you, we'd have our *brioche*.

12
You showed no great interest in your grandson
and hated any grandmotherly role.
The very appellation seemed to appall
you, as if threatening your sense of fashion
and proper distance. No cuddly fat munchkin

hugger you. It was all about control
and self-possession and your ghastly will.
The touch you craved was near another ocean
under the calm fingers of your masseuse.
What you could buy you could put trust in—
even to that huge, sombre library
whose books you never bothered to peruse.
You were just out there like the last Victorian
dying amidst some phantom tea party.

13
With enough money nothing need be real.
You blew through seven hundred thousand,
a grand a month for your group psychic plan
alone. The rest, just baubles of the *haute* genteel—
Cartier clocks, drawers full of identical
designer suits in three sizes, not one
worn—scarves and sweaters numberless as sand,
and so on. Mostly it was pretty dismal
being you those last years, ordering things
through UPS. to have a moment's friend
when packages arrived. Your eyes were failing
and liver functions—clear rememberings
of things that had not ever happened.
The sirens in your blood-starved head were wailing.

14
When it was clear the money had run out,
quite willessly you fell upon your sword,
refusing Laesix that your doctor ordered
and losing him for that. For one coquette
moment you tried to call a quick about
face, change your mind. Nurses were guarded—
it was too late now for that. You looked bored
and drifted back to sleep. And that was that.
Your new friend-cosmetician held your hand.
Another startled as she entered your room
and one bright blue eye held her in its death-chill.

There was no code blue or shenanigans.
You'd become bride to yet another groom.
The angry child kicking in your head lay still.

15
Your portraits we brought home filled several boxes—
from Shirley Temple days to the young Hepburn,
your slightly cocked head and cocked eyebrow turn
the gaze inward, despite the outward glances
at the demanding camera. Long eyelashes
veil the quick bright eye. Something flickers and burns
and smolders out. A certain porcelain
veneer distracts us from your beauty's darkness.
What you held dearest was your inner kingdom.
In most all of the portraits, that shows up.
None of them hold the look I cherish—
that devil-may-care, slightly-over-the-top,
what-the-hell grin. That wink. It all said come
dance, little broody boy, it's all there is.

Invocations

My steps slower than I would have imagined
even in summer

who once could not help but run
Crimes I've done myself I would not undo

Cicadas in a tree singing
the dappled 'out there'

the shrill of birdsong

* * *

Sands of the desert and sun warm me
and I forgive my pederast father
and remember his shy laugh

Spawn of East Texas swamps snakes on the brain
Stink of rot and piney woods loneliness
Bible-belt mom dowsed in lavender

I had an engineer's hat like my grandfather's
high in the sun-flared locomotive squinting into the light

the two of us until the whistle blew
and he was a crouched old man on a hospital inner tube

My father's bones shattered like glass and he died
worse than a dog so I forgave him

remembering his shy laugh glints of gold
in his long old teeth

Two funny stories maybe three and no one knew him
His skull in death an old Ojibwa's

* * *

At night the familiar hocus pocus of moon and mind
You soft in shadow that other
I know myself by

Come Light warm me
Sit on my grandmother's shoulder
who reads me through measles and chickenpox
bringing the world and New Orleans
in two blue suitcases

Light on the banana tree tallest of grasses
Light in her hazel eyes

* * *

Salt sand of the desert the long unfolding white of it
Out there I stole my bride from the land of the untouchables
Spirit me away dawn of the cockcrow
Light of my wavering window

* * *

My one great photograph you naked on a chaise lounge
eight months pregnant sleeping in the sun
light circling your circles
and one long draped arm

Light of the moment and always

* * *

Our son came out a greased chicken when he was born
and shone in the light of all subsequent Christmases

He seemed too small to take home
I had to learn to hold his head up

Your breasts engorged made you the gaudy
fertility goddess carved on a wooden salad spoon
I remembered from childhood

I gave him his first bath
Danced him heart to heart
Happy on the high hill of our summer

* * *

And happily I am already dead in a book somewhere
but in the dark closed pages or the light of a window
I don't know

To think I was ever a blank page
a tabula rasa a salt flat
a star

Hold the light at the window I am coming
though my knees ache

* * *

I have always enjoyed near the Equator
how sun maps a face
though I live in the snow

I was young in the sun of tennis courts
Pure form and goat mind
fencing the air

before the flat-light green-haze of hospitals
moon men in surgeries
Mother a mirage in the midnight
arriving from Rome

Stars of Paris outside my window
The girl I held in the dark for 13 years
against my loneliness

swims in the sun of the Pacific now
or is dead

* * *

I made love on a red cliff over the Mediterranean
at midnight in the cove of Los Pinos
to a woman from another language
beautiful as a mermaid
and hairy as a 23 year old
I was young dumb in a hurry
No star touched my soul

* * *

When I think of light I think of salt flats or snow
though its jewels in the leaves are delectable
and fire your black hair

All these summers I've watched you garden our gold hill
Your hillocks not bad Old Woman
raised like prayer

Names of flowers elude me unless I look them up
Is it the desert in me or a dark mind
that cannot name these belles of light

My first garden was elephant ears and banana trees
and blunt nosed tortoises I kissed on their blunt noses
mossy bricks of the patio
a slight breeze I still recall
on my heat-rashed two-year-old naked buttocks

At three and a ward of the Church
I wanted to bathe with the Deacon's
13 year old daughter Mary Katherine
because I liked her pubic hair
how it swirled in the warm water

One or two baths and everyone thought better of it
From then on it was Morgan or Hank

And still my life seems strange
I think my lake the Danube sometimes
or remember the pale lime-thick turquoise of the Karoon River
an eel under my left foot
in a shock of wonder

Salt flats and snow and the gardens between

*   *   *

Wherever it was light wanted to go
I said Yo Dis here is America
Let's do-si-do
Dat old Walt Whitman he big he kind
but boring

Which tribe am I
The twang the drawl the Yankee clipper
Which thrum of weathers
Which codes and netherworlds
Which beestings on the tongue

Or is the eye my alibi
and crude syntax

*   *   *

The eye that travels
sees still waves from airplanes
thunderless beaches

In the border towns
of the dead and nearly dead
comes dawn's bleak windows

The casualties were
entirely justified
say the generals

And all that flat line clarity is light

But what of the gutturals of evening
the festooned flesh and ornamental slang
the topsy-turvy muscles of a million mutabilities
carnal carnivals and carnivores
boardwalk bazaar bodega
heartstrings of the tongue's thrumming

when light of the blood is a kind of light

* * *

I drummed through the booze jungles of Bangkok
at age 15 door to door whore to whore
till one just 17 took me home to meet the folks
and wash me in the kitchen sink
It was intimate chilling a grim mirror
and in the sickly light of the bare bulb
she was truly beautiful
How much of her may have wished to dance
on my grave I don't know

* * *

Angels and vaginas the angels are
vaginas says my sculptor friend in his studio
when I find his new seraphim
stock and static

Stepping back I see it
Yes
if thighs had wings surely we could fly

From a dark declivity a few curlings
broadening into fern fronds
and baroque arabesques
a vertical mouth for a trunk
and the tree of life is any man's wife

* * *

And then there were the horses of the sun
ablaze over the clattering rooftops of the world
or at least Khuzistan with its rock hills
and smugglers' trails
A heart beat between the knees
A breathing like the very wind
Flying the flags of themselves in their girlish manes
the foolishness of all our fathers in their wild eyes

In a monoprint I bought from a friend
three horses graze in a pasture
that might be cloud
the passionless horses of dream or a far field
closer to me now than the horses of wind and fire
muscle and bone
though I miss their salt scent
the rivers of sweat mapping the veins of their necks

Or maybe my friend's print is a dream of horses
dreaming their pastures dreaming their clouds
dreaming the artist dreaming of horses
whose absence is light
around the dark remembered bodies

* * *

When my horse the fastest in all Khuzistan died
I was away at college and knew in an instant
my childhood had ended
I tried writing a poem

but couldn't get the Braille of his skin
under my fingers onto the page
He'd lent me the great thunder of his body
and I had lain on his flanks in his stall while he slept
We loved each other with humor like brothers
On the day of our triumph he had blown by
Star of Persia to win by 20 lengths
He nickered and snorted when he heard my footsteps
and when I did not come for months he died
His life blessed mine as only animals can bless
Sometimes our betrayals are mindless as wind
and a man moves emptier than the child that had been

* * *

Moon of my mind with your long black hair
Come nearer sit opposite
Let me paint you the girl in the rattan chair
one full breast exposed
one knee drawn up that hides the other
A portrait in shadow but the light of the room

Or now the wise handsome woman Penelope old
whom Odysseus fears taking his eyes off
in his fog of years
The firm cool cheek and coolish eyes
and fires that flicker at night
along her spine

Flesh is not sexy to an old man's eye
until defied by gravity the slightly
slipped buttocks that affirms some pride
the waist loosening its stays
that still has grace
the back that arches that's known some ache
Of course it helps he knew the girl
entwined back in that Ithacan Eden world
neither of them doin nothin
that wouldn't make her mama's hair curl

* * *

The song of the desert is the song of oases
the white sand and midnight blue
of Persian Miniatures

In college I took the Luscher Color Test
"not a party game" we played
as a party game

The colors you chose showed your balance of mind
the book said and I got four asterisks
which meant not even with psychological counseling
would my mind be right

I saw the cultural bias of course
bright yellow and cool green
being the colors of Switzerland on a nice day

I chose burnt orange and a warm brown
the colors "only refugees" had chosen
the colors of Iranian cliff towns

Third I chose a dark blue
which meant according to the book
I used sex to block my fears
of various underworlds and my sense of doom

O well
The pipes of Pan play
as the pipes of Pan do

And it was a midnight blue
the color of oases
the cry of loons

* * *

In a glaze of light
the desert men of the high plateau
have faces like worn shoes
Descendents of Alexander's men
their gazes impassive over wide valleys
their stories as cadenced
as Omar Khayyam

Goats jangling like temple bells
they take tea in a circle
talk with their hands
haggling the prices of horses

I know nothing of their wives
or daughters
shadowy sometimes giggly in the doorways

* * *

No massing of light on a sundown cliff face
was ever more magical than the changing light
in our son's face

The garden gnome crouching at your side
primed to know name and each thrilling step
of each new planting his voice
of query and awe a small
very silvery bell

His little collie Tommy carved trails
into our deep thickets and taught him the woods
quail raccoon an occasional fox
 a big black stray he glowered down
like the wrath of God
He died on one of those trails on a sunny day
at just age 10 with a single yelp
Our son's wail like a knife in the heart
lasted forever

What could I teach him the world
is sometimes like a poem but mostly isn't
Distrust money men corporate slogans pompous diction

The larger he grew the smaller I seemed

Now he has sideburns like Jim Bowie
and slouches in the sun where he walks

We hope he'll learn to think

* * *

I wanted to write a poem
whose first line anticipated its last
a box of inevitability
an inevitable box

But life is not like that
Life is a Bob Dylan song
that might go anywhere
or become mumbly and indecipherable

Tramps train whistles a bad sky

We wait for the refrain
Buzzards are circling the bad sky
Tramps enter the train whistles
and then the far blue mountains

But we have faith
Beauty is also circling we think
We wait for the refrain

* * *

And there you are again in the garden
after long winter and long years

your sports car body our chiropractor
complains you treat like a truck
your mud wife duds a swatch of black earth
glazing your forehead
radiant
pensive
dreaming garden again out of the squalor
of sticks and mud the sprawled
scrawled skeletons
There's no light I'd rather enter
than this sun on our porch in late March
the bare trees on the far hills rusting with inner fires
the lake ice jagged and scarred
and about to vanish

And we could vanish too Love
become wolves on our ancient hill
our tails still plumed and playful
our eyes still fires

a little blood on the sumac leaves
their wands waving toward a new autumn

Vilnius Glimpses
For Kornelijus Platelis

In the lonely room of the poem

(sifting
plaster dust
and spreading wall
maps of moisture
in the slow
garlic-sour crumble
of old Europe)

the heavy-faced poet ponders the book of losses
dreaming redemption
from the irony and ache of arthritis

or maybe the clatter and clash of sun-bright weapons
as the pagan suicide knights of the forest
vanish into the blood-smoke incense
of the crucifix

but no let up in the relentless walk of the world
eyes dead ahead
ghosts of the mind cops and word killers

and too little mystery or amnesia
in a quart of *degtine*

no matter the glassy glitter of boutiques
no matter the smart fashion-girls with their cell phones
and small taut buttocks

and the roaring poets of cavernous taverns
blinking into the sun
to mumble poems like apologies
in the still sacred tongue of oak and linden

and placating shrines to the gothic gods of unmaking—
rampant St. George plunging
his lance into the waiting mouth of the monster
and interchangeable saints
wilting like flowers

I want to go home to make love
to my beautiful wife
on the timeless hill of our dreams
stolen from the Iroquois

I want to tear out my teeth in the soundproof
torture chambers of the KGB
and forget the cool-eyed women cut down
in the demystified forest
like a thousand Dianas

I want words to unsay themselves
and the clocks to stop

I want to drink till I drop
and sleep in the gutter
with the rain leaking into my brain
and be washed in the blood
of inscrutable gutturals
and make a friend of sorrow and terror

I don't want to be written into the heavy book
of the poet with his bitter grief
and Sphinx-like gaze
knowing it all might have been otherwise

though our eyes have met
and there's no going back

Lamentations

Lament 1

I sat on the edge of my bed and I wailed and I wept
and I wanted to be empty as wind
and avoid all this old man dying shit
all this piecemeal dissolution humiliation
I wanted to rise like the Phoenix like the sun
and be new in the morning like the sun
I wanted to be 56 forever everything still
almost possible you like a mirage
just ahead within reach a rainbow's
shimmering I wanted to walk in
content in my fate to be walking still walking
the ache in my knees both telling and reassuring
and you in the paper tiara from the party
Queen May aswirl in the ribbons of mock death
and resurrection and I knew making love
 to you would make me whole through the universe
and everything else the denouement the terrible denouement
weeping and keening holding the rags the bitter rags
and then I was empty as wind and quiet

Lament 2

I went to the place of the poem but it was small
and dark and smelled like the ancient dens of foxes
Time kept coming back to scratch at the door
Old words littered the walls as if to keep the damp out
Someone had lit a fire but the ashes were cold
and the spiders were everywhere
And there was such sadness in the spaces between words
so much nothingness in the everything they said
Why fear the nothingness but we do
How fear the meaninglessness which we are
Here is my voice hang it on a tree
Here is my shoe which remembers me

And beautiful were your black diamonds
like the beauty of the sea at night
the points and spires and breezes of the night
where you passed and I followed and the words went out
and I vanished

Lament 3

I wanted to steal the last word from Death I suppose
and the silkiest of thefts are the poems of moonlight
poems of the sea and vast deserts their premonitions
And yet the Angel of Death is all kindness we're told
leading us out into moonlight through cracks in the clouds
had we known had we listened as the terrible talons
of pain and undoing let go
                        let us pray let us hope
the last ravening moments no end of consciousness
but a beginning
              let us hope let us pray
though your buttocks domes against my limp gizmo
are all I need tonight to shore me home

Lament 4

How shall I say goodbye to myself poor
Charles Bon in his New Orleans and his emptiness
his decadence and charm and poisonous knowledge
who yet found you beyond all luckiness or fate
Goodbye to the heart hurt by its own betrayals
the mind full of inconsequence and error
a voice too full of itself
knickknacks and charms and the color blue
the silent cries of trees and the lake's sheen
and the numberless leaves haunting the numbered days
The man of the hour is the skeleton in the sombrero
who lies down in the curves of the voluptuous senorita
to a clatter of bedpans in the wings and the cackling of the damned
I sang you the songs of your fiery bones

and the soft opening flower of a dying kiss
Farewell to the grief of days and the holy smell of roses
your face knees voice like water
thighs like snow and eyes full of sky
Your laugh startled me so so so long ago
My will such as it is I give to clouds and to dreaming
my bones to the cathedrals of sand
to the pottery shards of lost places
my eyes to the vulture who resembles me
my wishes to wind and my loneliness
to thousand year old trees and the deserts of desire
I loved you in the simplest of ways my girl
and this is my poem which has no ending

Lament 5

I can imagine the loneliness of widows unraveling
unwelcoming days and old men in shut rooms
measuring their meds losing their minds dates names
If only vanishing were easy an old movie maybe
the corny deathbed speech the melodrama
each bedside mourner a cameo and case study
You see it in the eyes the soul speaking eye
to eye for the last time drinking the last horizon
And the faces strange and the rooms we wake in
with a start the floor moving and the windows dark
are no more ours than the clouds are or the voices of children
Is it the book misplaced that makes me weep
or tortured animals slaughtered children rape
by bayonet or any gone world's going
My grandmother kept a book 85 years pressing
a four-leaf clover given by a friend when they were five
Isn't that worth more than walking on the moon
but nothing stays still straight or in place
but the mute dignity of bones
bones without memory bones without song
So let us go under the hill and over the sky
and let us be bones together

The Dark Mothers

are wailing for their lost sons.
For them little has changed since Moses
but the weapons. A grief ago, the desert wind,
the on and on relentless drone

of once soft women in the murmuring grass
now crones of the hard afternoon light.
Lizard skin and hands become bird claws,
unforgiving eyes, like the mirrors of time.

Keening out of the dark towns of my past
the dirges of the young undone
in their animal prime, the I-in-eye
vanishing in the caldrons of oblivion
where once Zarathustra dreamed.
    +   +
I planted for the goddess some small conifers
now taller than our house and touching the stars,
one a great monster swaying in the moonlight
like the headdress of Shiva
swaddling a dozen birds, a million crawling things.

Together we dance on forgetfulness
and the clouds become elephants.
So this is old age, where the light splinters and the dream
ricochets, and the so-what bird laughs
like Rembrandt's last self-portraits.

(But the poet wants only to speak of sky and the ocean
of sand, to point to the setting sun
with a shrug of indifference.)
    +   +
The weight of the dead is in the weightlessness
of the vanished who gave you dimension.
The 8th-grade teacher with a Boston accent
who says repeatedly don't call me ma'am,

the east Texas "mammy" with a face like Louis Armstrong
who carries in her sainted flabby arms
the first skewers of guilt and self-loathing,

and so on and so on with the vanishing weight of being,
the slow dissolution of knowing and caring—

the stone door, the widow's wail,
the click of the lid.
  +   +
And so she brings fire to the ragged dark
in the flare of her hipbones,
swirl of her thighs. Tapering fingers
seamstress nimble, spidery smooth.

And now your absence glows
in the vaults of her belly, toss of her hair.
The slippery dark dances. But already
she is elsewhere, tomorrow
or yesterday, phantom of your best self
curling into smoke—dawn inventing the near hills,
the charred black of your face bones

wobbling back into morning.

Winter Light

> *Like a long-legged fly upon the stream*
> *His mind moves upon silence.*
> —W. B. Yeats, "Long Legged Fly"

He was only the pale winter light
listening. He was old.
The woman had come, shimmering
like a tree reflected in water, and given him eyes.
Now she was fading back into forest
where he could not follow. She hated
his dreary naps, lies. Eternity yawned
into the wavering salt flats of his youth
that had meant distance and loneliness
and something he could not name,
yawned into the land of the dead
where all the old ghosts stood like statuary
with no need for names. His mind
the black edge of a crow's wing,
it had been a long winter, a white desert.

He was listening.

* * *

                    Armies on the move again
and the rice bowls empty. Bodies in the mountains,
bulging in rivers. A small man, unhoused
in a small boat, trying to save his skin.
In the palace a little wine under the indifferent
beauty of sky, a little sex, a little death.
And the stink of it, rape and the mad dance
among fires.
                Li Po trudging the hills far from home.

* * *

As if the sky itself were sluicing down
into their slumberous bodies: blue horses
in an orange field ablaze in late sun,
a kind of paradise of the moment, out of time
and therefore holy. At the edge of the field
a shadow, the menace of time. Or is it
the face with many lines gazing from the window
into the fragrance of horses, the draped manes
and long faces of peace in the grass, skin
that rippling makes the whole body smile.
The woman had shown him this, in her broad hips
and liquid thighs, the chime of her laugh.

* * *

He imagined the upthrust cathedral's burden of stone
poised impossibly on a mathematical notion,
moonlight streaming down through the clerestory—
all that blood soaked stone aching to be light,
or if not light, wings—
voices glancing off stone muffled in the tall air,
officious whisperers, assorted saints, She
off in a corner encaved in her forest of stone,
only the Mother of God now,
not of the trees and grass.

* * *

The Oneidas tell their stories only in winter
so that the snakes who hide behind leaves
cannot hear them—the way poems are made
so the thugs lurking behind walls
with their electronic gadgetry
grow blank as river stones.
In dreams I return to the hill people's
fires and drum circles, speaking my poems
to the dark full of sparks and fireflies.

A woman lay down like a black river there
in the moonlight drunk with poets.

* * *

He came on the rank river of swarming humanity
and beautiful ochres
to the gold temple with its leafy chimes
pearling the air like the voices of insect angels—
the pumpkin headed, pumpkin colored monks
anonymous as flowers—
a place of exact thoughtlessness
stirred by a single tremulous note
like the smile of the sky itself.
Overhead in the voluptuary trees,
the white fanged, long tailed gods and goblins
chuckling like monkeys—
in the time before time in the reign of the tiger.

* * *

He dreamed these things as the wind blew and the cold deepened
and the shadows behind his face
became a gathering of crows arguing with evening—
each caw a vanishing soul, each coal-black eye
ironic and insolent. Praise be
to the nefarious crow—carrion eater,
squawker, complainer—
Praise be to our allotted cup of blood.

Once
—with some thefts from Simin Behbehani

I came to you as if from a far country
The night was not quite in your eyes
but the evening smoke and the roses of your skin
met in purple shadows

I came through the vague veiled streets
toward some clarity or hunger
You were my fire in the moth-light
my confessor

You danced the stars blind under the witching moon
I crawled in your darkness like the tapping beetle
Our mouths met

Dawn in the desert is a million gold butterflies
I lived there once among broken stones
husks of bodies
a tale of death and deaths
and women turned to salt
under stubborn hummocks of black cloth

We grow old like the cracking clay
of forgotten rivers
Soon no one will remember our voices
or the glancing light of our tremulous
tremors

Was it the wind I came on
lipping your waters
combing the sunlight scarves across your throat

So often now we are tired
and old women I once knew speak softly
behind the curtain

and the mud of the riverbank
squelches under their feet

I came through bulrushes over moon-glazed bayous
and our bodies became snake-dancing
cranes
feathery cries

We cannot love each other forever
except as the stars do
all flame and nothingness

Our skins will grow worn and frail
as papyrus leaves
locust wings
May the burden of pain bring lightness

We lie down to take flight
like the desert sand under the scour of wind

I came like a sea eagle out of the sun's eye
to whirl you talon in talon
down the roller coaster sky

I met your gaze in the forest of being

The rest was just history

www.ingramcontent.com/pod-product-compliance
Lightning Source LLC
Chambersburg PA
CBHW031136090426
42738CB00008B/1106